THEN   NOW

HYANNIS

OPPOSITE: Hyannis's location on Nantucket Sound and its sheltered harbor made it a busy port, but it was the beauty of its seascapes and sailing ships that kept drawing back vacationers from northeastern cities year after year. (Historic image courtesy Hyannis Public Library.)

HYANNIS

Janet M. Daly

To those residents of Hyannis and Hyannis Port, who, for almost 400 years, have weathered with warmth and wit the winds of change in this beautiful seaside village as both year-round or summer vacationers, I dedicate this book with love and respect.

ON THE FRONT COVER: Pres. John F. Kennedy gave Hyannis and Hyannis Port international cachet when he selected his family's compound as his summer White House. The museum bearing his name draws people from all over the world to discover and remember his presidency in the old but refurbished 1926 town hall. (Historic image courtesy the *Barnstable Patriot*.)

ON THE BACK COVER: The Hyannis Public Library is an example of Hyannis's community spirit, and to this day, it welcomes both young and old to sample the knowledge found in books, newspapers, and magazines as well as the Internet through WiFi, CDs, DVDs, and e-books. (Historic image courtesy Hyannis Public Library.)

CONTENTS

ACKNOWLEDGMENTS

There is a long line of dedicated men and women who deserve our thanks for preserving the history of Hyannis and Hyannis Port in word and especially photographs from the mid-18th century to the present.

They include the staff at the Hyannis Public Library; the dedicated archivists at the Sturgis Library who have digitized the *Barnstable Patriot* and other early journals through 1930; residents who saved photographs, including those from the Newman collection/Old Hyannis Port; and David Stills III, the current editor of the *Barnstable Patriot*, who opened his photographic files to make this book as complete as it is. We don't know the names of many photographers of the past, and although they are anonymous, their contribution to our knowledge of this village is significant. Alvah H. Bearse's book *Physic Point: Memoirs of Hyannis 1914–1929* was especially helpful because of the map that "placed" houses, churches, and commercial buildings in situ.

The idea for this book was planted when the Hyannis Public Library scanned photographs from a scrapbook in the archives and librarian Ann-Louise Harries recognized their significance. With the help of her successor, library director Carol Saunders, other photographs, old maps, postcards, and memorabilia were reviewed. Then, Friends of the Hyannis Public Library decided to take on the job of compiling a book comparing photographs of the past with present-day ones. I was fortunate to be the one to head up the endeavor, designed to acknowledge the library's historic collection, and to provide royalty revenue for its coffers.

Jennifer Longley's book *Hyannis and Hyannis Port* in Arcadia's Images of America series was the single most important source of the village's photographic history. She was also most generous in steering us in the right direction when we reached dead ends.

Extensive research in those old newspaper archives; the commemorative booklet of the town of Barnstable, *Barnstable at 350*, published in 1989 by the Barnstable 350th Committee, which provided a very thorough timeline; and the library's cache of booklets on various village institutions were most important to someone who did not grow up in Hyannis and had to piece together where various landmarks and buildings no longer extant were located. What surprised me and confused me was how many different buildings have sat on one site over the many decades covered in this book!

The generosity of dozens of people in the community was essential to the creation of this book. I have been asking almost everyone I meet about the village since I began my research, so I have chosen not to list any names for fear I will forget someone. You all know how much I appreciate your time and memories, and so I offer my profound thanks and hope you will understand my discretion.

Finally, as an amateur photographer but a person who loves to discover old buildings hidden behind new facades and to see how the landscape has changed over the years, I enjoyed every minute I have spent working on this book and hope you enjoy reading it.

Introduction

Hyannis is the largest of seven villages that comprise the town of Barnstable on Cape Cod in Massachusetts. It serves as the Cape's "big city," with a first-class hospital, a community college, a major shopping center, and the largest concentration of restaurants and entertainment outlets in the area. It has all of this, plus the great American hometown treasure of a "Main Street, USA."

Hyannis is also a major tourist destination. The local chamber of commerce says it is a "hot spot" village that draws tourists and residents because of its beautiful beaches, wind, and wonderful waters for sailing and swimming and because the 35th president of the United States, John Fitzgerald Kennedy, made it famous as his summer White House 50 years ago.

Historically, its sheltered harbor on Lewis Bay first attracted the early settlers, and its seaside location has over its long history continued to bring people to its shores. The Hyannis and Hyannis Port area was purchased by colonists from the Cummaquid sachem Yanno around 1664. (Hyannis is derived from the sachem's name, which is often spelled Iyannough or Iyanough today.)

Hyannis has always welcomed diversity, unlike other Cape villages. English, Irish, French Canadian, Spanish, Portuguese, Cape Verdean, Native American, and African settlers have found a home in Hyannis. What drew them originally was the sea. Whaling, fishing, and merchant ships provided jobs. Some farming, especially the cranberry bogs, also drew residents, but the harvest that brought the most money was shellfish—like oysters, clams, and lobsters—and cod. By 1750, Henry C. Kitteridge noted in his *Cape Cod: Its People and Their History*, "the Cape had become largely a maritime region."

During the Revolutionary War, this meant that many seafaring men were privateers, using merchant ships armed to fight the British. But while the war also hampered trading outside the region, coastal schooners kept commerce thriving along the Atlantic Coast. From 1815 on, saltworks and dried cod provided prosperity to both landowners and seafarers. The 1850s were the height of good times in maritime Hyannis and on the Cape.

The commemorative booklet *Barnstable at 350* noted the following: "Hyannis assumed maritime importance during this time. Largely because of its Hyannis Port breakwater, constructed at a cost of $400,000" around 1826. The port and its wharf, which later became the railroad wharf in 1854, "became one of the most important harbors of refuge on the Eastern Seaboard," reported a newspaper of the day.

For 30 years, ship captains from the area thrived during the golden age of sail. Their homes were built along the tree-lined streets of Hyannis and its port, and many survive to this day providing historic references to the past.

By 1850, Hyannis was the hub of the Cape, and the coming of the railroad in 1854 had it touted as a future "favorite summer resort." Thus began the development of summer colonies of cottages for the wealthy living and working in the Northeast. A boom was forecasted. What resulted was a bust. The Civil War ended the age of sail, as steam-driven Confederate vessels plied the coastal waters of Cape Cod blowing sailboats of Union sympathizers out of the water. The great division of North and South hampered industry in the nation, causing a financial depression. The discovery of underground salt in New York also halted the lucrative retrieval of salt from the seas around Cape Cod.

However from 1860 through 1920, Hyannis residents chose to look locally and established churches, schools, and libraries and became active in social, religious, educational, and fraternal organizations.

The railroad may have replaced the sailing ships and the automobile the horse as methods of transportation for business and pleasure, but it also spiked renewed interest in vacationers and those seeking a summer home. It was during this time, in the mid-1920s, that the Kennedy family first arrived in the area. Joseph and Rose Kennedy first rented and then purchased a house, which was the beginning of the Kennedy Compound in Hyannis Port. They were an example of the affluent young couples with large families who spent their summers sailing and swimming on the Cape. Their offspring became enamored with the area and continue the tradition to the second and third generations.

When war came to the Cape, Camp Edwards and its Otis Air Force Base brought Americans from throughout the country, who were as charmed by the area and its assets as earlier tourists. When the war ended, the picturesque quality of Hyannis, coupled with its very active social amenities, made the village a favorite spot for young adults. Many found seasonal employment at the many inns, hotels, and resorts.

Not only were people able to travel to Hyannis via railroad, automobile, and bus but also by plane because there was now an airport, too.

Then came the election of John F. Kennedy to the presidency and his summer trips to Hyannis Port. The crowds grew even larger, and tourism became the preeminent industry.

Today, the Cape has a large and growing retirement population that enjoys its resort lifestyle while benefiting from established institutions such as a symphony, theater groups, churches, libraries, adult education, golf courses, a highly respected hospital, and all the amenities of a city with the charm of Main Street, USA.

CHAPTER 1

FROM SAIL TO RAIL IN THE 19TH CENTURY

The Civil War and the rise of steam power sent Hyannis's sailing industry into steep decline. But steam powered the railroad, which reached Hyannis in 1854 and brought tourists to the seaside village. The depot sat in the center of the fledgling business district, and railroad tracks crossed Main Street. (Historic image courtesy Hyannis Public Library.)

South Hyannis Lighthouse was originally a private enterprise built in 1848 by entrepreneur Daniel Snow Hallett. When a federal light was erected, Hallett became its first keeper. Decommissioned in 1829, the lighthouse remains a reminder of Hyannis's age of sail. Adjacent to a private home, the lighthouse stands sentry today as ferries, power and sailboats, and excursion and day-fishing boats leave and enter the harbor. (Historic image courtesy Hyannis Public Library.)

Old Colony Railroad Depot jutted out into Main Street, with the tracks diagonally crossing the street. It was the village commercial center in the late 19th century. The Universalist church steeple is visible in center background. Every building, including the church and all structures to the depot, were destroyed by fire December 3, 1904. Today, a concrete triangle marks the depot site, and the Federated church steeple rises into the sky. (Historic image courtesy Hyannis Public Library.)

Nantucket Steamer Service began in September 1854 when a railroad spur was continued on to the railroad wharf. Service was discontinued in 1872 when the railroad reached Woods Hole. Small coastal packets still carried products along the coast and to the islands through the 1900s. Today, there are no wharfs or coastal vessels; summer vacationers are able to enjoy Sea Street beach and look out on a small jetty, which probably contains rocks from the wharf. (Historic image courtesy Hyannis Public Library.)

Around 1870, a railroad crossing sign marked where the railroad tracks bisected Main Street. A man and dog seem unworried by any traffic from either horse or railroad. A lantern man's hut is on the near side of the tracks and was used when trains crossed the street. John Norris's bakery is at left. Today, a streetlight keeps automobile traffic in check. The old track bed is now paved over as Old Colony Way. (Historic image courtesy the *Barnstable Patriot*.)

Hyannis Park was developed after the turn of the 20th century thanks to the Old Colony Railroad, which provided regular transportation to the seaside. Skirting the southeast shore of Hyannis Harbor, the development is actually in Yarmouth, but developers thought the Hyannis name was a bonus. Today, some original homes remain, and several have added porches or been enlarged. The Hyannis beach in the foreground provides close-up views of pleasure boats and ferries plying the harbor. (Historic image courtesy Hyannis Public Library.)

Cottages Hyannis Park, Hyannis, Mass.

Pres. Ulysses S. Grant stood before Cash & Bradford store on Main Street to address townspeople during the congressional campaign of 1874. Here, Myron Bradford, standing on the step at left, and Alexander Cash, seated next to him, posed with friends. The Boston Store, visible at right, was where the March 4, 1892 fire started. Both businesses were destroyed. An apartment house and Bradford's Ace Hardware are on the site at Main and Pleasant Streets. (Historic image courtesy Hyannis Public Library.)

The day after the Cash & Bradford/Boston Store fire, townspeople survey the devastation. Across the street, stock rescued from the stores is piled on the snow-covered ground. Alexander Cash's house can be seen through the still smoking wreckage. He rebuilt his store as the Cash Block in 1893. The Congregational church and Crowell's shoe store are visible. Today, Main Street remains busy. Commercial buildings have replaced both the church and store. (Historic image courtesy Hyannis Public Library.)

The Cash Block replaced the buildings of the Boston Store and Cash & Bradford at Pleasant and Main Streets after the 1892 fire. Cash Block contained Myron Bradford's hardware business, a shoe store, dry goods store, and post office. A bowling alley, pool hall, and barbershop were in the basement. Today, Bradford's Ace Hardware occupies the entire building and is one of the oldest continually operating businesses in Barnstable, since 1892. (Historic image courtesy Hyannis Public Library.)

Daniel Crowell's shoe store, located next to the Congregational church (note its arched windows) on Main Street, offered custom footwear. The First National Bank of Hyannis moved to this building in 1866. In 1894, the bank relocated to its own building. During the 1920s, the Crowell Building was connected to the Hyannis Inn, run by William Cox. Today, a large three-story commercial building stands on the site. (Historic image courtesy Hyannis Public Library.)

Main Street around 1895, east of the depot visible in the background facing west toward the railroad tracks, shows part of Daniel Crowell's store, the Congregational church, Alexander Cash's home, and the rebuilt Cash Block. Today, only the Cash Block remains. The Church Bell Building, where the first car is parked, was built on the site of the church, which accounts for its name. Small shops are on the street level. (Historic image courtesy the *Barnstable Patriot*.)

Capt. Sylvester Baxter's house was where 14 village women brainstormed with Baxter's wife, Rosella Ford Baxter, about forming a public library. The house was built in 1855 and added to the National Register of Historic Places in 1987. In the Park Square neighborhood on east Main Street, it was once the Park Square Inn. Today, the old Baxter house with its distinctive cupola is painted pink and is the Park Square Village apartments. (Historic image courtesy Hyannis Public Library.)

Park Square around 1915 was a large triangular park located where tree-lined Main Street branched off to the left and to the right, Park Street was one way to Hyannis Park. Today, the triangle has been significantly reduced. Park Street was shortened and is now accessible only from Lewis Bay Road, which crosses Main Street and leads to Cape Cod Hospital. Park Square is the site of the town's World War I Memorial. (Historic image courtesy Hyannis Public Library.)

0710   Main Street & Park Square,   Hyannis, Mass.

Main Street around 1905 was residential on the south side, but on the north, a market occupied the corner house with the Odd Fellows Hall next to it. Today, the former Hibel Museum Building and the second Masonic Hall, now shops and apartments, are on the south side, with the Gateway Building on the north where the market was. The Odd Fellows Building, enlarged with a new facade, is still on its same site. (Historic image from Hyannis Public Library.)

Main St., Hyannis, Mass.

From the Baptist church at High School Road looking east, Main Street around 1895 was lined with elm trees and fine residences of sea captains and local merchants. Fences were necessary in residential areas, and where there were no gates, waist-high posts were installed to prevent horses with carriages from wandering onto front lawns. Today, the only horsepower propels cars down Hyannis's Main Street. (Historic image courtesy the *Barnstable Patriot*.)

The Octagon House on South Street was the home of sea captain Rodney Baxter, who built the home with 18-inch-thick concrete walls in 1855. It was designed by Orson S. Fowler, who advocated for eight-sided houses in his book, *The Octagon House, A Home for All*. Today, the house and its matching octagon carriage house stand almost hidden from view by towering trees. In the 21st century, the house remains a private residence. (Historic image courtesy the *Barnstable Patriot*.)

Shown around 1903, Murphy's Ice Cream Wagons delivered this popular 20th-century treat right to people's homes. William T. Murphy was proprietor of an ice cream shop and catering business located on the north side of Main Street near Barnstable Road. He also bought John Norris's bakery, which was across the street and on the other side of the tracks. Today, Tommy Doyle's and the Mayflower Shops, built in 2011, occupy the site. (Historic image courtesy Hyannis Public Library.)

Hyannis's First Hotel, built in 1832 by Capt. Charles Goodspeed, was purchased in 1854 by Evander White. He named it the White House. With the 1872 land boom, he sold it to the Hyannis Land Company for offices and accommodations. In memory of the Indian sachem for whom Hyannis is named, the company called it the Iyanough House. Before demolition in 1935 for the Cape Cod Times Building, it was known as the Ferguson. (Historic image courtesy Hyannis Public Library.)

The Masonic Temple was built in 1855 next to the White House hotel. Its first floor was the venue for plays, concerts, entertainments, and dinners. The Masons met on the second floor, where Obed Brooks also ran a school in a back room that was reached by outside stairs. It was "a building filled with memories of our social life" well into the 1930s, according to historian Clara Hallett. TD Bank is now on its former site. (Historic image courtesy Hyannis Public Library.)

A normal school was built in Hyannis in 1896 because it was considered Cape Cod's trading center. There was a railroad, "a national bank, a good hotel, a printing office, a library and reading room, about thirty stores, and four churches," according to a 1922 history of the school. Also included was a training school, far left, and dormitory, far right. Today, the Barnstable Town Hall is in the school building. That is Sachem Yanno marking the Walkway to the Sea. (Historic image courtesy Hyannis Public Library.)

Fire struck the school's campus on January 24, 1896, destroying the new Hyannis Training School, just two weeks after the grammar school opened. Local school buildings, emptied on completion of the training school, were brought back in use to house the students. A year later, 204 elementary school students through the eighth grade returned, three months after the normal school and dormitory welcomed its first class. Today, the Verizon communications company is located at this site. (Historic image courtesy Hyannis Public Library.)

The Saturday Night Club (S.N.C.) Building was just across Main Street from the depot. The two stores in the building were Chase & Wright Millinery and William Lovell Jr. Clothier and Furnisher. A library reading room sign connected the S.N.C. Building and attorney John Bodfish's office next door. Today, the building, now the Furman Building, is seeking new tenants, and Persey's restaurant, famous for serving breakfast all day, is in Bodfish's office building, which has enlarged and added a facade. (Historic image courtesy Hyannis Public Library.)

Shops within homes were still commonplace in most villages as the 19th century came to an end. The house at left, adjacent to the Baptist church on Main Street, is a perfect example. Today, the building remains at the same location. The porch has been enlarged and enclosed, and architectural details have been emphasized thanks to a multicolored paint job. It houses Kandy Korner, where both villagers and tourists stop to sample "penny" candy, including delicacies from the 19th to the 21st century. (Historic image courtesy Hyannis Public Library.)

Summer visitors of the 19th century traveled via the railroad to the Cape to enjoy the cool breezes, sun, and sandy beaches, which were as appealing back then as now. Hyannis, Hyannis Port, and the islands were the destinations then as now. But today, Hyannis's Transportation Center is a modern bus terminal linking travelers with Providence, Boston, New York, and their international airports. Today, taxis and local bus service have taken the place of horse-drawn livery. (Historic image courtesy Hyannis Public Library.)

FROM SAIL TO RAIL IN THE 19TH CENTURY

CHAPTER 2

AUTOMOBILES BRING PROGRESS IN THE 20TH CENTURY

The railroad propelled Hyannis forward, as sail gave way to rail. This peaceful 1903 streetscape, with horse-drawn carriages and about two dozen stores, would soon change drastically. Fire would destroy the church and stores right up to the depot. Automobiles would drive horses out to pasture, and air travel would begin to take off. (Historic image courtesy Hyannis Public Library.)

On December 3, 1904, the worst fire in Hyannis's history destroyed the Universalist church, post office, and all the stores on the north side of the street east to the railroad. The church complex went up in flames. Scorched earth and ashes of 14 other buildings lined Main Street. Today, the Federated church, formed when the Universalist and Congregational churches merged in 1917, stands on this site. (Historic image courtesy the *Barnstable Patriot*.)

VIEW OF RUINS OF BUSINESS SECTION OF HYANNIS, DESTROYED BY FIRE Dec. 3 1904.

Published by Walter D. Baker, Hyannis, Mass.

Within a year, all the shops destroyed by fire were rebuilt, except for the post office. One of the old schoolhouses located on west Main Street was moved to house it, third from left, and a new facade was constructed. It opened in April 1905. Other stores included Megathlin's Drugstore, Robbins Dry Goods, Baker's Department Store, and Wilson's Public Market. A Brazilian congregation, three restaurants, and a photographer are located here. (Historic image courtesy the *Barnstable Patriot*.)

American Clothing House was a long-running clothing store on Main Street, founded in 1885 by Louis Arenovski, an immigrant who started his business as a peddler. He ran this clothing store well into the 20th century, and sold real estate from an office over the store. Just two doors east of the Masonic Lodge, the lot is part of TD Bank's large corner location that runs to Old Colony Way. (Historic image courtesy the *Barnstable Patriot*.)

AUTOMOBILES BRING PROGRESS IN THE 20TH CENTURY

Hyannis Patriot is the sign on this Pleasant Street building around 1906, which was when the *Barnstable Patriot* relocated its entire headquarters to Hyannis. Hyannis was fast becoming the communications hub of Cape Cod. The separate Hyannis edition, which was first published in 1890, was discontinued in the 1940s. Today, this 1830 building houses McEvoy Media, which deals in 21st-century communications. The building is in the National Register. (Historic image courtesy the *Barnstable Patriot*.)

A World War I troop train, with 164 Cape Cod young men aboard, is about to depart for Camp Devens on September 23, 1917. Family and friends surround the train, while officers wait to embark. Today, no passenger trains leave the station. Instead, Cape Cod Central Railroad takes people on scenic excursions, some including lunch and dinner, on the old railroad route to the Cape Cod Canal in trains from a similar era during tourist season. (Historic image courtesy the *Barnstable Patriot*.)

AUTOMOBILES BRING PROGRESS IN THE 20TH CENTURY

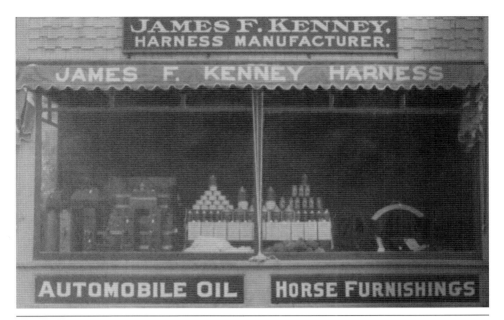

Harness maker James F. Kenney realized the automobile would replace the horse, and his store window reflects this. Kenney did not desert his old customers; he instead branched out to owners of automobiles too. Kenney's shop was in the Odd Fellows Building on Main Street, west of Ocean Street. Today, Ben & Jerry's ice cream store is in this location, catering to those on foot or who come by automobile. (Historic image courtesy the *Barnstable Patriot*.)

No one seems to be the owner of this c. 1914 automobile, which is truly broken—or its wheels are at least! Since the mishap occurred in front of Richardson Brothers Photographers, it is highly possible the photograph is from that studio, which was located on Main Street east of Ocean Street. Today, the Federated church and a Thai restaurant are located here, and automobiles line Main Street. (Historic image courtesy Hyannis Public Library.)

AUTOMOBILES BRING PROGRESS IN THE 20TH CENTURY

Connolly's Garage on Center Street, just off east Main Street, features gasoline pumps, a repair shop, and Chevrolet automobiles to purchase around 1920. Chevrolet's bow-tie logo on the sign debuted about this time. Today, the bus line Plymouth & Brocton Street Railway Company, established in 1888, has a large garage and maintenance shop in this location. There is some similarity of the rounded marquee facade on both buildings. (Historic image courtesy the *Barnstable Patriot*.)

A welcome home parade, led by local women's groups, came up Main Street from the depot on July 4, 1919. Veterans from World War I were returning, and the town celebrated their homecoming. Today, Hyannis still loves its parades and uses the same parade route to this day. Shriners are shown riding miniature vehicles in this parade, which followed their convention held in 2011. (Historic image courtesy Hyannis Public Library; now image courtesy the *Barnstable Patriot*.)

AUTOMOBILES BRING PROGRESS IN THE 20TH CENTURY

The Odd Fellows Hall is decked out in red, white, and blue bunting. Shown are Mr. and Mrs. Thomas Carroll, proprietors of the antique shop, who share the first floor with James F. Kenney Harness Manufacturer, who also sells automotive products. Hyannis's Main Street shopping center had expanded west to Winter Street around 1919. Today, a brick facade transforms the building, which houses shops that sell ice cream and skateboards with the Odd Fellows located upstairs. (Historic image courtesy Hyannis Public Library.)

Silent movies came to Hyannis in 1913 with the opening of the Idle Hour theater, which was one door up from Ocean Street on the south side of Main Street, just across from the Odd Fellows Hall. There were seats for 500. After two fires in the 1970s, it was torn down. During the summer of 2010, a mini-golf course was built to benefit Barnstable High School extracurricular activities. (Both images courtesy the *Barnstable Patriot*.)

Eagleston Inn was on Main Street at Bassett Street in 1915 and was owned by James Eagleston who sold it a decade later to Morgan S. Dada. It was a seasonal hotel that catered to wealthy visitors who could enjoy the inn's famous chicken and lobster dinners, see fashion previews, and check out their stocks at Pillsbury, Remick & Co.'s summer offices. Today, a block of stores is located at this once bucolic corner. (Historic image courtesy Hyannis Public Library.)

Mayflower Hotel opened in July 1926 on Main Street near Stevens Street. There were 70 guest rooms, a Packard chauffeur service available, and a Paine, Webber & Co. office. Although the financial crash occurred in October 1929, the hotel remained a popular seasonal hotel until the 1950s, when it was demolished. Today, a smaller commercial building has been built there as part of the rebuilding at the west end of Main Street. (Historic image courtesy Hyannis Public Library.)

The Hyannis Inn was a popular hotel for traveling salesmen, who arrived in town by railroad and wanted a central location near the depot. In 1914, a fire provided the hotel's owner Charles Nye an opportunity to expand by connecting with the old Crowell shoe store building. William Cox acquired the hotel and added to the original structure in the 1920s. Today there is no trace of the inn, but a motel occupies the location. (Historic image courtesy the *Barnstable Patriot*.)

The 400 Main Street building was the centerpiece of a pre–World War II Hyannis. An upscale Main Street evolved during the Roaring Twenties to serve the affluent tourists and second homeowners who visited from Memorial Day through Columbus Day. Year round, it was also the Cape's shopping center. Today, the building remains Main Street's commercial anchor with the Naked Oyster restaurant, Puritan Clothing, the *Barnstable Enterprise*, and a scrapbook/craft shop. (Historic image courtesy Hyannis Public Library.)

The Hyannis Theatre opened in 1924 with 900 seats. It featured the only orchestral pipe organ on Cape Cod useful for the vaudeville staged with movies in the 1920s. There was also a ballroom upstairs and shops on the first floor. Today, the building's exterior remains intact, painted a lighter color softening the Tudor beams. There is a street-level restaurant and shops, with the upper floors converted into condominiums. (Historic image courtesy the *Barnstable Patriot*.)

Megathlin's Drugstore was a Main Street fixture, rising from the ashes of the 1904 fire. By 1925, it had grown into a drug and variety store, anchoring a shopping area with Bassets Bros. grocery, the post office, Baker's Department Store, and Wilson's Public Market lining the street. Today, Megathlin's building is a Christian church serving the Brazilian population. Next door is Fazio's, and a photographer has a studio in the old post office. (Historic image courtesy the *Barnstable Patriot*.)

AUTOMOBILES BRING PROGRESS IN THE 20TH CENTURY

1103—U. S. Post Office and Town Office, Hyannis, Cape Cod, Mass.

PHOTOGRAPH BY HARRISON FISK

OB-H1871

Hyannis Post Office 02601 was part of Pres. Franklin Roosevelt's Works Projects Administration. The building was located adjacent to Barnstable Town Hall, creating an anchor for Hyannis's Main Street. It was built by the Treasury Department's public buildings program in 1937 and is still in use today as one of the busiest post offices on Cape Cod. The JFK Museum, at right, is now in the old town hall. (Historic image courtesy Hyannis Public Library.)

Ushering in passenger air travel to Hyannis, the original airport had a single grass runway when it opened in 1928. The Town of Barnstable took over the airport in the 1930s, and it was commandeered during World War II for use by Navy aircraft on antisubmarine patrol and for pilot training with three 4,000-foot runways. Today, Air Cape Cod heads up private aviation facilities in roughly the same location. (Historic image courtesy the *Barnstable Patriot*.)

Cultural
Landmarks and
Institutions

This 1884 map of Hyannis shows its rural nature with some of its first churches, many of which remain today. The railroad depot (A) is at far left; the Universalist church (H), now the Federated church, is at center right; the Baptist church (J) is at top right; and the Catholic chapel (K) is at bottom right. (Historic image courtesy Hyannis Public Library.)

The Baptist Society was founded in 1771. In 1825, a meetinghouse with a bell and clock tower was built on Main Street at High School Road. The photograph was taken around 1895. Today, the church cemetery in the rear of the property has tombstones from 1800. The church is in the heart of the village; its clock is a community timepiece. There are church tours and a thrift shop as well as devotional services. (Historic image courtesy the *Barnstable Patriot*.)

The Federated Church of Hyannis was founded in 1917 when the Congregational and Universalist congregations merged. Three churches have been on this site. Shown is the second Universalist Church built in 1905, following the 1904 conflagration. The Congregational church was farther east on Main Street. It survived the 1892 fire but was demolished for commercial buildings. Today's church was built in 1958 but has been added to over the past 50 years. (Historic image courtesy the *Barnstable Patriot*.)

St. Francis Xavier Parish was formed in 1902. Before then, Catholics attended St. Patrick's mission founded in 1872. A church was built in 1904 on South Street, which has been expanded four times since. Today, the church holds 900 people and has tours for visitors who wish to see where JFK worshipped. St. Francis Xavier Prep School is part of the complex. Sunday masses are offered in English, Latin, Spanish, and Portuguese for its diverse congregation. (Historic image courtesy the *Barnstable Patriot*.)

CULTURAL LANDMARKS AND INSTITUTIONS

Hyannis Public Library, formed in 1865, moved to 401 Main Street in 1908, after operating on Pleasant Street. The house, dating back to 1830, was Postmaster Otis Loring's home and office. Capt. Samuel Hallett purchased the house in 1840. When he died, his heirs sold it to James Otis who gave it to the library. Today, two successive additions dwarf the historic house, half of which operates now as the library bookshop. (Historic image courtesy Hyannis Public Library.)

The Asa Bearse House was a Main Street landmark restaurant during the 1980s. It was built in 1840 by a sea captain. In 1879, Dr. Samuel Pitcher, who invented the patent medicine Castoria, made it his home. On his death, it became the Beechwood Inn. The site has been home to a variety of restaurants over the years. Today, it is being renovated into a restaurant featuring Brazilian cuisine and sophistication. (Historic image courtesy the *Barnstable Patriot*.)

CULTURAL LANDMARKS AND INSTITUTIONS

Hyannis hospital, seen on the far left near the corner of Sea and Main Streets, had been Lindsey Oliver's home. Members of the District Nursing Association ran the first hospital, established in 1910. An ad noted it welcomed convalescents and those who were ill and mentioned a fully equipped operating room. It closed when the Cape Cod Hospital was opened in 1920. Today, the Windmill Square shopping center stands where Victorian homes once stood. (Historic image courtesy the *Barnstable Patriot*.)

Cape Cod Hospital was opened in 1920 with 14 beds in Dr. Edward Gleason's former home overlooking Lewis Bay. In 1924, the Ayling Wing was opened, adding 31 more beds. Today, Cape Cod Hospital is a 259-bed acute-care hospital, one of America's top 100 hospitals. As a regional medical center, it employs 1,700 staff and 300 physicians. There have been three more additions; the latest is the five-story Mugar Building at left. (Historic image courtesy Hyannis Public Library.)

Barnstable Town Hall offices were moved to Hyannis's Main Street from Barnstable village in 1926 when a modern two-story brick building was dedicated. As the town grew, more space was needed for administrative offices, so they moved to the building of the old normal school. The John F. Kennedy Museum was opened in the old town hall building in 1993. The sculpture by David Lewis depicts JFK walking through beach grass. (Historic image courtesy the *Barnstable Patriot*.)

The Hyannis Fire District was established May 6, 1896, and was the first one of the Town of Barnstable's districts. The action was taken in response to the January 24, 1896 fire that destroyed the training school. The first firehouse was at the rear of Keveney's store on Main Street, near Center and Elm Streets. In 1925, the department moved to 44 Barnstable Road at Elm Street. Today, an insurance firm occupies the building. (Historic image courtesy Hyannis Public Library.)

CULTURAL LANDMARKS AND INSTITUTIONS

High School, HYANNIS, Mass.

Barnstable High School was built in 1905 off South Street at the end of what is now High School Road. During the 1920s, when Hyannis built its new town hall, a brick high school was built on the same site. The building became a middle school when today's Barnstable High School was built in 1957. On September 4, 2007, the only Cape Cod Catholic high school, Pope John Paul II, opened at this location. (Historic image courtesy the *Barnstable Patriot*.)

The Barnstable Police Department moved into this brick building on Elm Street in 1926, located close to the Hyannis Fire Department. The police were responsible for all seven villages. Today, the department occupies a modern complex on Phinney's Lane and Route 132. The old police station is now the Mid-Upper Cape Community Health Center, providing affordable health care to the Cape's diverse population, including residents who speak English, Brazilian, Portuguese, and Spanish. (Historic image courtesy the *Barnstable Patriot*.)

CULTURAL LANDMARKS AND INSTITUTIONS

Cape Cod Synagogue held its first High Holy Days service at the Grange Hall on Louis Street on September 9, 1934. From 1938 to 1948, the congregation used several venues around town. In 1949, ground breaking ceremonies were held on Winter Street, the site of the present building. Today, the synagogue has been enlarged twice, first in 1979 and again in 1982. A green renovation has just been completed. (Historic image courtesy Cape Cod Synagogue.)

In the 1950s, a modern terminal was built to serve the growing number of passengers traveling to the Cape and Islands. In 1981, the name was changed to Barnstable Municipal Airport-Boardman/Polando Field, honoring Russell Boardman and John Polando, who trained at the field before their historic 48-hour flight to Turkey in 1931. Today, a new terminal and tower are slated for completion during 2012. (Historic image courtesy of the *Barnstable Patriot*.)

CULTURAL LANDMARKS AND INSTITUTIONS

First Church of Christ, Scientist Hyannis conducted its first service on July 3, 1949. It was a consolidation of the two older Christian Science churches from Cotuit and West Yarmouth. Located on Bearse's Way and Stevens Street, the two buildings were moved from Cotuit and settled on new foundations, creating the new assembly complex. Over the years, the buildings were joined to create more space, and further expansion and modernization have continued over the years. (Historic image from First Church of Christ, Scientist.)

Zion Union Church officially came into being in 1962 as an interdenominational congregation after being a Baptist mission church since 1909 on North Street. In 2003, a building fund campaign was begun, and a new and larger church opened in 2006 on Attucks Lane. Today, the old building is now the Zion Union Heritage Museum, celebrating the African American and Cape Verdean population as well as other ethnic diversity on Cape Cod. (Historic image courtesy Zion Union Heritage Museum.)

CULTURAL LANDMARKS AND INSTITUTIONS

The Hyannis Yacht Club was originally located on Lewis Bay near the present Steamship Authority terminal at the end of Pleasant Street. The first clubhouse was dedicated in 1896 and was sold in 1938 when a new building was erected off Ocean Street, adjacent to Veterans Park Beach. The clubhouse has been enlarged over the years. It includes the Captain's Table restaurant and has an attractive pier for its members. (Historic image courtesy Hyannis Public Library.)

Barnstable's town offices were moved from the 1926 building in 1979 to the normal school built in 1896, which ended the building's history as a college. A teacher's college until 1944, it was the site of the Massachusetts Maritime Academy until 1949. Cape Cod Community College moved in for a decade. Today, Town Hall looks as fresh as when it was first built thanks to a complete restoration of its exterior. (Historic image courtesy the *Barnstable Patriot*.)

CULTURAL LANDMARKS AND INSTITUTIONS

CHAPTER 4

POSTWAR CHANGES

Residential building took off after World War II as GIs home from the war began families. Five dozen duplex houses were built off Bearse's Way, at right, for young families as starter homes in 1945. The development provided much-needed affordable housing for Barnstable County residents, whose numbers doubled from 1940 to 1970. (Historic image courtesy the *Barnstable Patriot*.)

Main Street Hyannis around 1950 epitomizes Main Street America of the time with automobiles lining the sidewalks on any given weekday. Blue laws had not been abolished at this time. This stretch of road opposite the library is "shopping central" for village residents as well as all of Cape Cod.

Today, trees almost hide the cupola that once topped the A&P, but all the buildings, including the 400 block building, remain along a now one-way street. (Historic image courtesy Hyannis Public Library.)

On the left corner where the *Barnstable Patriot* offices are now, the Fish Store once held sway. Across Ocean Street and down one building, the marquee of the Center Theater is visible. Across the street, the Hollywood Gift Shop had taken over the old Woolworth location. Now, the theater is gone, the corner building across Main Street was refaced, and small shops line the avenue, which is still a one-way street. (Historic image courtesy Hyannis Public Library.)

Main Street, Hyannis, Cape Cod, Mass.

The Cape Cod Melody Tent was started originally as the Melody Circus in 1950 by Broadway producer Richard Aldrich and his actress-wife, Gertrude Lawrence. It was located first on North Street in Hallet's Field. Later, it moved to its present location on West Main Street. Now a nonprofit, it is the site of star-studded "theater in the round" performances by headliners such as Tony Bennett, Huey Lewis, and the Temptations. (Historic image courtesy of the *Barnstable Patriot*.)

Hyannis Firefighters battled the inferno that caused great damage to the Center (once the Idle Hour) Theater. It was located on the south side of Main Street, with Golub's on one side and Cape Cod Travel Agency on the other. The theater was subsequently torn down. Today, an empty lot is all that is left of Hyannis's oldest movie theater, and Jack's Drum Shop replaced the travel agency. (Historic image Gordon Caldwell photograph courtesy Hyannis Fire and Rescue Department.)

The intersection of Main Street and Old Colony Way, shown around 1960, was a construction site as old gave way to new in the form of the Cape Cod Bank & Trust Company Building. At far right, a cleaners has replaced the railroad buildings. Today, all but one of the buildings on Main Street remain. TD Bank now occupies the old CCB&T Building, and the Hyannis Transportation Center looms at right with the scenic railroad at far right. (Historic image courtesy the *Barnstable Patriot*.)

Sightseeing by boat became popular with John F. Kennedy's election in 1960 as tourists wanted to see the Kennedy Compound and this was the best way. Hyannis Harbor Tours was founded in 1962 at the Ocean Street pier. Fishing excursions and ferry service to Nantucket and Martha's Vineyard were added over the years. Now operating as Hy-Line Cruises, there are state-of-the-art boats for all three services and a modern terminal with two restaurants. (Historic image courtesy of Hyannis Public Library.)

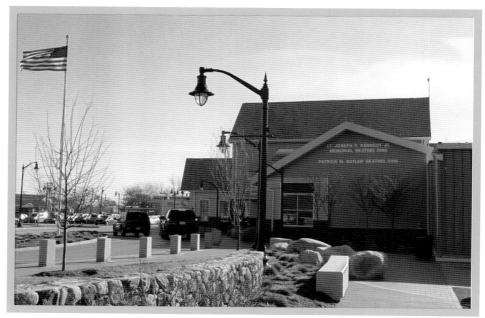

Lt. Joseph P. Kennedy Jr. Memorial Skating Rink was donated in memory of President Kennedy's older brother, who died in World War II. Originally built as an open-air skating rink in 1957, the rink was enclosed in 1967. The last public skate was March 22, 2009, and afterwards, the structure was demolished. A rink in Lieutenant Kennedy's name is now located in the new Hyannis Youth and Community Center. (Historic image courtesy the *Barnstable Patriot*.)

The Hyannis Holiday Motel was located on Ocean Street, facing the harbor. It was just one of many motels built during the 1960s and 1970s to accommodate the influx of seasonal visitors to Cape Cod's hub. Today, the Hyannis Harbor Hotel is at this location, just across from the Hy-Line Terminal and a rejuvenated harbor front complete with artist's shanties and new harbormaster's offices. (Historic image courtesy Hyannis Public Library.)

The John F. Kennedy Memorial was built in 1966 by the people of Barnstable in honor of the 35th president of the United States who made his summer home in Hyannis Port from 1926 until his assassination in November 1963. The memorial is on Ocean Street and overlooks Lewis Bay, waters JFK loved to sail. It has changed little today, except that adjacent to it is the town's Korean War Memorial. The JFK Museum is within walking distance. (Historic image courtesy Hyannis Public Library.)

CHAPTER 5

HYANNIS PORT AND THE KENNEDYS

Hyannis Port's beauty in 1872 influenced the Hyannis Land Company to purchase waterfront property from Dunbar's Point to Centerville, plus Squaw Island. Lots were staked, and homes and hotels were built to lure vacationers and homeowners. By the end of the 19th century, Hyannis Port was a posh summer resort for millionaires from the Northeast. (Historic image courtesy Hyannis Public Library.)

The Stoneleigh Gables was a Hyannis Port hotel for over 50 years, offering water views from 1905 until it was demolished during the 1960s. Located at the corner of Irving and Longwood Avenue, the hotel was just a short distance from the Hyannis Port Yacht Club, which is just visible at the end of the road. Today, private homes occupy the location just across the street from the Kennedy Compound. (Historic image courtesy Hyannis Public Library.)

THE GABLES, HYANNISPORT, MASS.

HYANNIS PORT AND THE KENNEDYS

Squaw Island Road around 1876 was muddy but well traveled. The building boom was in full swing, and dozens of large summer cottages dotted the island. Local population and industries—sailing and saltworks—were declining, but the seashore attracted more people who brought money earned elsewhere. The resort era had begun and continues today. Squaw Island remains a wealthy enclave. JFK rented homes there in 1962 and 1963 for greater privacy. (Historic image courtesy Hyannis Public Library.)

Around 1890, Hyannis Port was dotted with windmills used to bring running water into the many homes and cottages built along the shore. Sailing was a popular sport and a pier is just visible at far left. The pier became a community meeting place for residents. Today, a much larger pier is the same for Hyannis Port Yacht Club members with both sail and motor boats. Eugenia Fortes Beach is in the foreground. (Historic image courtesy Newman collection/Old Hyannis Port.)

The Landmark is what they called the tall structure at far right in this c. 1900 photograph of Hyannis Port's East Beach. It was called this because sailors at sea used it as a navigational aid. It actually was built as a water-pumping station. Today, the tower, now the studio-shop of impressionist artist Sam Barber's waterfront compound, remains a familiar sight to sailboats off Hyannis Port. (Historic image courtesy Newman collection/Old Hyannis Port.)

Founded in 1897 as the Hyannis Port Golf Club, the Hyannisport Club, pictured around 1910, had shortened its name in 1909. John Reid, the Scotsman who helped introduce golf to America, designed its front nine holes. The September 1944 hurricane, which devastated Hyannis Port, demolished the clubhouse. It was rebuilt with a dining room. Today's clubhouse has been enlarged over the years, with even tennis courts added, but it still enjoys panoramic views of Nantucket Sound. (Historic image courtesy Newman collection/Old Hyannis Port.)

HYANNIS PORT AND THE KENNEDYS

St. Andrew's by the Sea is an Episcopal church that was completed in 1911 at the top of Sunset Hill. Prior to its construction, Episcopalians had services at the Union Chapel. Adjacent to the Hyannisport Club, the church grounds offer compelling views of Hyannis Port, the golf course, and Nantucket Sound. Today, the church is open in the summer for 9:00 a.m. Sunday services and marked its centennial year in 2011. (Historic image courtesy Newman collection/Old Hyannis Port.)

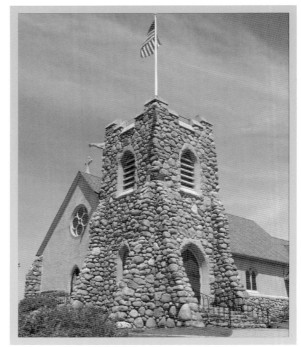

The original Union Chapel was built in 1890 in the heart of Hyannis Port but was destroyed in the hurricane of 1944. Timber from the old church was salvaged and used to construct a new church that was completely different in design, with a tall spire and classic New England church lines. Today, the chapel is little changed from when it was rebuilt over 60 years ago. There is a 9:00 a.m. Sunday service during the summer months. (Historic image courtesy the *Barnstable Patriot*.)

This Hyannis Port streetscape around 1910 shows a variety of summer cottages and several windmills, which marked the skyline of Hyannis Port in the early 20th century. Today, the house left of center remains unchanged, but the homes on the right have been enlarged and are just visible behind the high fences. Tourists eager to get a glimpse of the Kennedy Compound nearby often make it necessary for residents to seek some privacy. (Historic image courtesy Hyannis Public Library.)

N STREET, HYANNISPORT, MASS.

Joseph and Rose Kennedy's home was purchased around 1926. Since then, it has been the family's summer residence. Joseph Kennedy died there in 1969 and was buried from St. Francis Xavier Church in Hyannis. His wife, Rose, was 104 when she died in 1995, the oldest Barnstable resident at that time. In August 2009, Sen. Edward Kennedy's body left the home after his death there. (Historic image courtesy JFK Library Foundation; now image Merrily Cassidy/the *Cape Cod Times*.)

Pres. John F. Kennedy's home on Irving Avenue, Hyannis Port, was purchased in October 1956 and became the summer White House during John F. Kennedy's presidency. It is owned now by Edward Kennedy Jr., the senator's son, who purchased it from Caroline Kennedy after her brother's death. Today, the house is barely visible thanks to mature trees and a stockade fence added after JFK became president. (Historic image courtesy Hyannis Public Library.)

Hyannis Port Post Office is shown with its flag flying at half-mast following the assassination of Pres. John F. Kennedy in 1963. Next door is the seasonal newspaper and candy store where JFK would take his children. It was less than a half mile from the summer White House. Today, the post office remains at the center of Hyannis Port life, and the variety shop is a popular destination for summer residents. (Historic image courtesy Hyannis Public Library.)

About the Hyannis Public Library

THE PUBLIC LIBRARY, HYANNIS, CAPE COD, MASS.   No. 410

For almost 150 years, Hyannis has had a free public library. In 1862, Rosella Ford Baxter conceived of the idea of a library for the village. She recruited 14 women, and the library was thus born as a community venture. In 1865, the library was officially established. It had various homes before moving permanently in 1908 to 401 Main Street, Hyannis, to a classic Cape Cod house with lovely grounds. It was purchased for only $2,500 from the famed James Otis of Hyannis Port, who had held the building in trust after purchasing it from the heirs of Capt. Samuel Hallett.

The first home of the library was in what used to be Freeman Tobey's store in the 1860s, which is now the home of a printing and media company on Pleasant Street. A few years later, the library moved to the Saturday Night Club Building, still located on Main Street, across from Hyannis Transportation Center and the Cape Cod Railroad.

After reaching its present home, the Loring-Hallett-Otis House (reportedly built around 1830), no major changes occurred until the Eagleston Wing, located to the right of the original entrance, was built in 1938. In 1974, a major expansion of the library was made with the Twombly Wing behind the old house. In 2008, the wing was completely refurbished thanks to grants from five local community organizations.

Over the years, the Hyannis Public Library has served the community, from presidents, scholars, and businessmen to fishermen and children. As technology changes our community worldwide, adding new and instant response and information, the library is changing as well, while maintaining a Cape Cod–village atmosphere and lifestyle, and investing in the future of our patrons.

That is why the Friends of the Hyannis Public Library took on the adventure of compiling photographs, postcards, and newspaper clippings to create a comparison of our community then and now! The royalties from this book will ensure continued proceeds to purchase the ever-changing media from which we learn, as well as educate and entertain ourselves.

Discover Thousands of Local History Books
Featuring Millions of Vintage Images

Arcadia Publishing, the leading local history publisher in the United States, is committed to making history accessible and meaningful through publishing books that celebrate and preserve the heritage of America's people and places.

Find more books like this at
www.arcadiapublishing.com

Search for your hometown history, your old stomping grounds, and even your favorite sports team.

Consistent with our mission to preserve history on a local level, this book was printed in South Carolina on American-made paper and manufactured entirely in the United States. Products carrying the accredited Forest Stewardship Council (FSC) label are printed on 100 percent FSC-certified paper.

MADE IN THE USA